ENGGA MICKENS

APOSTLE & PROPHET OF GOD

As an Apostle and Prophet of the Most High, God, I am thankful for the privilege to scribe the revelation He revealed about the Bride of Christ. While in the secret place, He led me to an intimate fellowship as His Beloved. Enjoy the revelation of being His Bride and discover our Jewish heritage during our Exodus to which I was awakened in January 2020.

INFO@ENGGAMICKENS.COM

COPYRIGHTS

Copyright © 2022 by Engga Mickens

All rights reserved. No part of this book may be reproduced, distributed, or transmitted in any form or by any means, including photocopying, recording, or other electronic or mechanical methods, without the prior written consent of the copyright owner, except in the case of brief quotation embodied in critical articles, review, and certain other noncommercial uses permitted by copyright law.

Scripture quotations taken from the Holy Bible, New International Version, NIV Copyright © 1973, 1978, 1984, 2011 by International Bible Society. Used by permission. All rights reserved worldwide.

Scripture quotations taken from the New King James Version. Copyright ©1982 by Thomas Nelson. Used by permission. All rights reserved.

Scripture quotations taken from the Christian Standard Bible. Copyright © 2017 by Holman Bible Publishers. Used by permission. Christian Standard Bible, and CSB ® are federally registered trademarks of Holman Bible Publishers. All rights reserved.

Scripture quotation taken from the Holy Bible. New Living Translation, Copyright © 1996, 2004, 2015, by Tyndale House Foundation. Used by permission of Tyndale Foundation Publishers, Inc., Carol Stream, Illinois 60188. All rights reserved.

Scripture quotations taken from TPT are from The Passion Translation. Copyright © 2017, 2018, 2020 by Passion & Fire Ministries, Inc. Used by permission. All rights reserved.

Image of the Jewish months and the Gregorian months credited to Hebrew 4 Christians of www.hebrews4christians.com.

Image of the Twelve Tribes of Israel credited to Conforming to Jesus of www.conformingtojesus.com.

The flag images permissive use by CC-BY-SA license by CREATIVE COMMONS CORPORATION. THE WORK (AS DEFINED BELOW) IS PROVIDED UNDER THE TERMS OF THIS CREATIVE COMMONS PUBLIC LICENSE ("CCPL" OR "LICENSE"). THE WORK IS PROTECTED BY COPYRIGHT AND/OR OTHER APPLICABLE LAW. ANY USE OF THE WORK OTHER THAN AS AUTHORIZED UNDER THIS LICENSE OR COPYRIGHT LAW IS PROHIBITED.

Glossary of terms credited to www.Wikipedia.com.

Glossary of terms credited to www.sabbathhouseinstitute.org.

Glossary of terms credited to www.sooj.org.

Glossary of terms credited to www.gotquestions.org.

Glossary of terms credited to www.Chabad.org.

Glossary of terms credited to www.biblegateway.com.

Glossary of terms credited to www.Hebrews4Christians.com.

ACKNOWLEDGEMENTS

First, I thank Yahweh for waking me up to discover who I truly am. I thank my Lord Jesus Christ for His Blood, redemption, and for introducing Himself as my Beloved, my Protector, El Sabaoth, my Advocate, and my Provider. I thank the Holy Spirit, my best Teacher, Counselor, and Intercessor. I also thank God for the angelic host who war, protects, and perform God's bidding.

I want to thank my faithful husband of 25 plus years, my friend, Kerry Mickens, for supporting and loving me through my journey. A Prophet's walk is not easy nor is it for the family, but it is worth it. I also want to thank my children, Kerry C. Mickens, and special thanks to Christian Mickens, my co-researcher for this book. I am grateful for each of you loving me through my convergence into the Apostolic Prophet God has ordained me to be.

I am thankful for my parents, who gave me life, love, and support. My mother, Gwendolyn Hall, and my father, the late Henry Rose. I appreciate my sister Marsha Jackson and best friend/sister Trina Allen with a host of family and friends who supported me during my life journey. Special thanks to my great aunt Cutie Mae Jordan who constantly spoke to me about God.

In addition, I want to thank all of the family and friends who cheered me on through life. I thank God for those who serve as second parents: my aunt Janice Smith and uncle Pastor KZ Smith, my grandmother, the late Mary Rose, my friend, Jacque Mays, and my friend, Sondra Baker. I am thankful for Sadie Walker who served as a spiritual mom figure and for those who were intercessors. Special thanks to my uncle James Rose for always reaching out and sharing the word of God and aunt Deborah Muhammad for being there for me as God led. Special thanks to her and my son, Christian for co-editing the book.

Last but not least, I want to thank my covenant partner, Prophetess/Evangelist Shirley Gordon, and destiny partner, Maggie Mayo, destiny builders Apostle Grace Cruz, Apostle Joe Joe and Autumn Dawson, and Apostle Cherika Spells. In addition, I want to express gratitude to Prophet Ruby Soliz and Seer Lyndra Stacker for being watchman. God brought them into my life to help birth what God has said concerning Kingdom assignments.

INTRODUCTION

My journey as a Prophet of God began when I woke up from a prophetic dream in January 2020. Shortly after the prophetic dream of an Exodus with an angel, the Lord God, and I leading large groups of people through high terrain, I was called to the Office of the Prophet and later to the Office of the Apostle.

Like other prophets, I was affirmed by a company of prophets and apostles. I was affirmed by Prophetess Tonie Noelle, the late Prophet Teron Smith, Apostle Bryan Miranda, Prophetess Melody Miranda, and Apostle Miranda Kwame. I had the pleasure of attending the Spiritual School of the Prophets for a year with the late Prophet Teron Smith who taught me the prophetic with an apostolic convergence. I was commissioned in December 2021 from Kingdom Harvest Alliance under Apostle Chuck Pierce. I was affirmed as an Apostle in 2022.

God consecrated me for His use. I pray you discern God's heart and love for the Bride as we exodus to our promised land. The prophetic poetry, psalms, will give you insight into where you are on your journey as the remnant or the harvest.

As you read, there are note pages to write what the Holy Spirit says to you as you conclude each month. The book is written in the order of the Jewish Biblical calendar months. This book can be read in one sitting or by the corresponding Gregorian month. You will discern which Jewish month you are in, understand the tribe, and prophetic blessing spoken over them, and the psalms God inspired me to write while in the secret place during the respective Biblical month.

I pray it blesses you and through intimacy with the Holy Spirit you began to scribe from the Father's heart what He is saying to you. Email me below if you want to share what the Lord is saying to you at info@enggamickens.com.

FOREWORD

BY APOSTLE TRACEE BARLOW

It is with great joy and prophetic expectation that I write this foreword for a woman of undeniable oil and unique prophetic grace—Apostle Engga. Though she has only recently come under my spiritual covering, there is a deep knowing in the Spirit that God has divinely orchestrated this alignment for such a time as this. There are some connections that are born out of familiarity, and then there are those that are birthed out of prophetic purpose—and this is the latter.

From the moment I encountered her sound and her heart, it was evident that she is one who walks closely with the Lord. She is not just a voice—she is an echo of Heaven, carrying the weight of the secret place and the rhythm of divine romance between the Bridegroom and His Bride. This book, "The Exodus Chronicles of the Bride," is not just another prophetic work—it is a sacred unveiling. A call to return. A call to awaken. A call to prepare.

These pages are soaked in prayer and saturated with encounter. Each prophetic psalm flows like a river from the chambers of intimacy, carrying the reader into the depths of bridal identity, heritage, and holy anticipation. This is not just poetry—it is prophetic utterance, scribed from encounters in the Spirit, and written for a generation that must rise and respond.

In an hour where the Church is being summoned from slumber into sanctification, this book stands as a trumpet blast to the Bride. It is a mirror to reveal who we truly are—called, chosen, and being made ready. Apostle Engga writes with a voice that is raw yet refined, prophetic yet poetic, gentle yet weighty. She invites you not just to read—but to respond. What I love most about this work is that it is not entertainment—it is engagement. It draws you into dialogue with the King. It stirs your longing for holiness. It reawakens your sensitivity to His voice. And it calls you out of spiritual Egypt and into your promised bridal destiny.

As one who is now honored to serve as her covering, I bear witness to the authenticity of her call and the purity of her pursuit. This is not someone who writes from performance—she writes from posture. She has been in the wilderness. She has walked through the Exodus. And now she is emerging with a scroll in her mouth and oil in her pen.

"The Exodus Chronicles of the Bride" is for those who are not satisfied with church as usual. It's for those who are yearning for more—more intimacy, more revelation, more transformation. It is for the Bride who is shaking off garments of weariness and compromise and putting on robes of righteousness, adorned with oil and readiness. So, I encourage you—don't rush through this. Sit with it. Pray through it. Let these psalms stir your spirit and renew your vow to the One who is soon to return. Let this book mark you, melt you, and move you. Apostle Engga, thank you for saying yes. Thank you for scribing what Heaven entrusted to you. Thank you for leading with reverence, vulnerability, and power. This is only the beginning.

To the reader, welcome to the journey. May your heart burn again. May your eyes weep again. May your spirit arise again. And may we all, as the Bride, be made ready.

With love, honor, and apostolic covering,

Apostle Tracee Barlow

Founder, Awakening Nations Global Network

TABLE OF CONTENTS

Author's Page	1
Copyrights	2
Acknowledgements	3
Introduction	4
Table of Contents	5
Jewish Months 1-4	6
Jewish Months 5-8	7
Jewish Months 9-12	8
Journey of the Exodus	9
12 Tribes of Israel	10
Abrahamic Blessing	11
Chapter 1 Nissan (Mar/Apr)	12
Chapter 2 Iyar (Apr/May)	18
Chapter 3 Sivan (May/Jun)	26
Chapter 4 Tammuz (Jun/Jul)	31
Chapter 5 Av (Jul/Aug)	38
Chapter 6 Elul (Aug/Sept)	43
Chapter 7 Tisheri (Sept/Oct)	48
Chapter 8 Cheshvan (Oct/Nov)	53
Chapter 9 Kislev (Nov/Dec)	59
Chapter 10 Tevet (Dec/Jan)	67
Chapter 11 Shevat (Jan/Feb)	72
Chapter 12 Adar (Feb/Mar)	80
Call to Repentance	87
Glossary of Terms	88

JEWISH MONTHS

NISSAN

IYAR

SIVAN

TAMMUZ

JEWISH MONTHS

 AV

 ELUL

 TISHERI

 CHESVAN

JEWISH MONTHS

9 KISLEV

10 TEVET

11 SHEVAT

12 ADAR

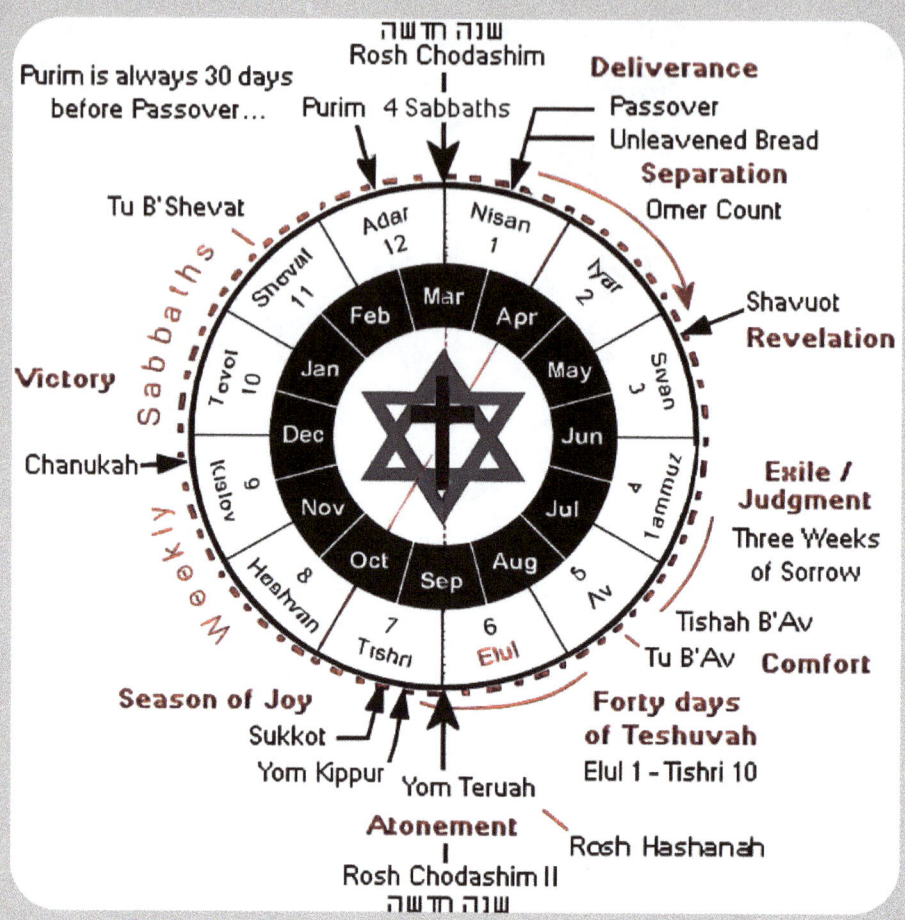

A VISUAL OF THE BRIDE'S JOURNEY

While discovering the roots of the Bride, I discovered there are two calendars other than the Gregorian calendar we use in the West today. The modern Jewish people use the Jewish Civil Calendar which is based on the months Jewish Biblical Calendar.

The Exodus of the Bride centers around the Jewish Biblical Calendar. The meanings of the months and seasons are based on the Jewish Biblical Calendar.

*Above image from hebrew4christians.com

THE 12 TRIBES OF ISRAEL

The Patriarchs: Abraham, Issac, and Jacob

Our father, Abraham, is the first patriarch who walked with God with tremendous faith. From his loins, came forth the chosen seed that would birth the chosen Bride. He began an Exodus with the Lord God, Yahweh. Abraham begot Issac and other children. Issac was the chosen son. Issac begot Jacob and another son. Jacob was the chosen son. Jacob begot 12 sons and all were chosen to possess the promise land. As we Exodus on our journey, you will learn of the twelve sons and their reward for obedience and their replacements due to disobedience.

The Patriarch Jacob 12 Sons

1. Reuben
2. Simeon
3. Levi
4. Judah
5. Dan
6. Naphatli
7. Gad
8. Asher
9. Issachar
10. Zebulun
11. Joseph
12. Benjamin

The Patriarch Jacob (Israel) Chart

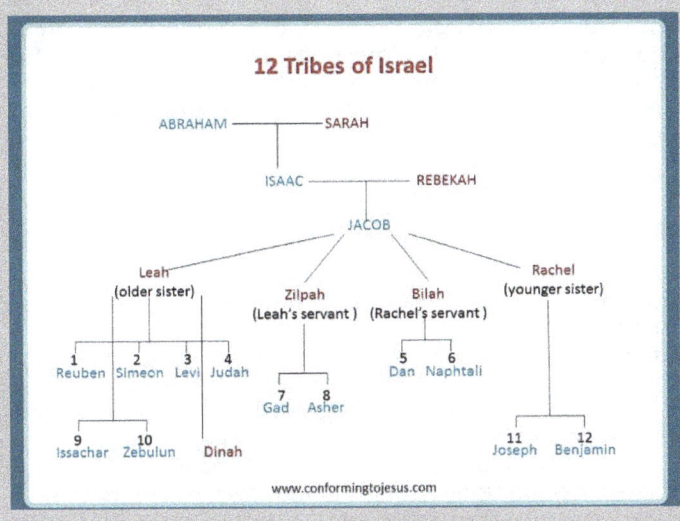

BLESSINGS
Abraham's Children of Promise
Yahweh's Blessing to Abraham

Genesis 12:1-3

1 The Lord had said to Abram, "Go from your country, your people and your father's household to the land I will show you. 2 "I will make you into a great nation, and I will bless you; I will make your name great, and you will be a blessing. [a]

3 I will bless those who bless you, and whoever curses you I will curse; and all peoples on earth will be blessed through you."[b]

YAHWEH, PATRIACH JACOB & MOSES' BLESSING TO THE TRIBE OF LEVI

The tribe of Levi is the priestly tribe. They are the priests of the Lord.

The Lord's blessing to the Tribe of Levi:

Deuteronomy 10:8-9

8 At that time the LORD set apart the tribe of Levi to carry the ark of the covenant of the LORD, to stand before the LORD to serve Him, and to pronounce blessings in His name, as they do to this day. 9That is why Levi has no portion or inheritance among his brothers; the LORD is his inheritance, as the LORD your God promised him.

Jacob's blessing to the Tribe of Levi:

Jacob's Blessing - Gen. 49:5-7

Blessing: None

"Simeon and Levi are brothers - their swords are weapons of violence. Let me not enter their counsel, let me not join their assembly, for they have killed men in their anger, and hamstrung oxen as they please. Cursed be their anger, so fierce, and their fury, so cruel! I will scatter them in Jacob and disperse them in Israel."

Moses' blessing to Tribe of Levi:

Deuteronomy 33:8-11

8 Moses said this about Levi:
"Levi is your true follower. He keeps the Urim and Thummim. At Massah you tested the people of Levi. At the waters of Meribah, you challenged them. 9 They were more loyal to you, Lord, than to their own families. They ignored their fathers and mothers. They did not recognize their brothers. They did not pay attention to their children. But they obeyed your commands. They kept your agreement. 10 They will teach your rules to Jacob and your Law to Israel. They will burn incense before you. They will offer burnt offerings on your altar. 11 "Lord, bless everything Levi has. Accept what he does. Destroy those who attack him! Defeat his enemies so that they will never attack again."

CHAPTER 1

THE MONTH OF NISAN (NISSAN)
MAR-APR

TRIBE OF JUDAH

The Tribe of Judah is associated with the month of Nissan. Judah goes first.

Nissan is the seventh month in the Jewish Civil Calendar and the first month in the Jewish Biblical Calendar.

MONTH'S SIGNIFICANCE

It is in this month that we celebrate the eight-day holiday of Passover.

PROPHETIC WORD

JUDAH PRAISE/WAR

THE LAST SHALL BECOME FIRST. TIME FOR JUDAH TO TAKE THEIR PLACE.

THE BLOOD OF JESUS WILL CAUSE US TO CROSS OVER INTO VARIOUS EXODUSES. DELIVERANCE.

TRIBE OF JUDAH (RUEBEN)'S BLESSINGS

The Patriarch Jacob (Israel's) Blessing

Jacob (Israel), the Patriarch after Issac, and Abraham, known as Israel, pronounced a blessing on Rueben as the first born but Rueben lost his position to Judah. Judah was Jacob's fourth son which replaced Rueben's tribe in the order.

Judah
Genesis 49:8-12

8 Judah, your brothers will praise you;
    your hand will be on the neck of your enemies;
    your father's sons will bow down to you.
9
You are a lion's cub, Judah;
    you return from the prey, my son.
Like a lion he crouches and lies down,
    like a lioness—who dares to rouse him?
10
The scepter will not depart from Judah,
    nor the ruler's staff from between his feet,
until he to whom it belongs[d] shall come
    and the obedience of the nations shall be his.
11
He will tether his donkey to a vine,
    his colt to the choicest branch;
he will wash his garments in wine,
    his robes in the blood of grapes.
12
His eyes will be darker than wine,
    his teeth whiter than milk.

The Deliverer Moses' Blessing

Moses led the children of Israel from Egypt. He pronounced a blessing over the tribe of Judah.

Moses' Blessing:

Deuteronomy 33:7

7 And this he said about Judah: "Hear, LORD, the cry of Judah; bring him to his people. With his own hands he defends his cause. Oh, be his help against his foes!"

PROPHETIC POETRY FOR THE BRIDE

I'm Standing. Wait and See!

I decree I am standing
with dried tears of love,
I am standing,
Waiting for manifestation from above,

I am standing,
No more prey to my enemies,
I am standing
No more looking for remedies,

I am standing,
For God, will come through,
I am standing,
in the promises which are from you,

I am standing,
until the glory fills this well,
I am standing,
Like an expectant person looking for the mail,

I am standing,
like a deer panting by the brook,
Who says I will go again to take another look,

No more mirage or fallacy,
No more hinderances, distractions,
to limit or delay me,

I am standing for my angels to assist,
as we wait for the expectant day of manifestation within our mists.

PROPHETIC POETRY FOR THE BRIDE

The Bride's Recompense

Lord thou art my recompense,
Thou art mine reward,
You've granted us to be your stewards,

How divine,
Remove the enemy at the gates,
Crush the head our enemies for Jesus' sake,

Our inheritance,
Our reward,
Oh, great Shepherd,

El Sabaoth,
Oh divine,
Expand your kingdom,
Reign down new wine,

New oil, pour out,
Living water from the spout,
Shout, Oh Bride,

For Judah is moving,
Shout and praise,
for glory will fall,
with force greater than Niagara Falls.

MY NOTES

CHAPTER 2

THE MONTH OF IYAR
APR-MAY

ENGGAMICKENS.COM

TRIBE OF ISSACHAR

The Tribe of Issachar is associated with the month of Iyar.

Iyar is the **eighth month** in the **Jewish Civil Calendar** and the **second month** in the **Jewish Biblical Calendar.**

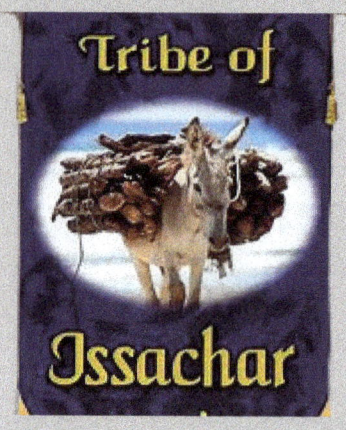

MONTH'S SIGNIFICANCE

Each day of Iyar represents another step in this spiritual journey towards Mount Sinai.

IYAR

PROPHETIC WORD

ISSACHAR tribe: Times and Seasons

We are awakened to the times and seasons.

Separation

TRIBE OF ISSACHAR'S BLESSINGS

The Patriarch Jacob (Israel's) Blessing

Jacob, the Patriarch after Issac, and Abraham, known as Israel, pronounced a blessing over his **12** sons. Israel's son, Issachar was the ninth son.

Jacob's blessing:

Genesis 49:14-15

14 "Issachar is a rawboned donkey
  lying down among the sheep pens.

15 When he sees how good is his resting place
  and how pleasant is his land,
he will bend his shoulder to the burden
  and submit to forced labor."

The Deliverer Moses' Blessing

Moses led the children of Israel from Egypt. He pronounced a blessing over the tribe of Issachar.

Deuteronomy 33:18-19

"Issachar is a strong donkey, Lying down between the sheepfolds. When he saw that a resting place was good And that the land was pleasant, He bowed his shoulder to bear burdens, And became a slave at forced labor."

PROPHETIC POETRY FOR THE BRIDE
The Bride's Wheat Season Pentecost

The Holy Spirit will reign and pour out His Spirit upon us.
We shall be changed into the resurrected mature version of ourselves from heaven to earth through the pouring out of His Spirit.
We will culminate into the present resembling Jesus.
We are the return of Christ.

As Sons of God, we too can occupy the earth for the dressing rehearsal of the lamb.
We will occupy in our glorified state.
Thanks to God the Father through the Holy Spirit.
No spot or blemish in our resurrected God nature.
No fear. Our temples will be better than the former apostles and do more works than Jesus.

We are created for this purpose to manifest as the Sons of God in the earth.
Expanding His kingdom while in heavenly places.
We are trained as Kings and Priests along with other offices to prepare for manifestation in the earth.

The harvest is ripe for others to make known the Kingdom is here.
They will be changed into the resurrection power of Christ.

We carry the anointing that destroys the yokes.
The Heir force, angels, warring angels, accompany us for every mission.

We walk with God's heart and spirit in total obedience and love.
The new creation springs forth with vitality and vigor!

PROPHETIC POETRY FOR THE BRIDE

The Five Wise

The Lord said, He is the beginning and the end,
He blotted out, washed away every wrinkle and spot of our sins,

The fuller's soap has done it's washing.
What is left is consecrated oil,
eternally lit and cleansed without soil,

He began a good work for all to see,
The breaker has gone forth with His redeeming blood and recompensed me,

I was not a foolish bride that some would presume,
preparing for my bridegroom,

Consecrating, recalibrating, and preparing for His promises may look unwise,
Walking and believing in the higher calling and for God's word to be fulfilled and arise,

Presumption is dangerous without the revelation of the Holy Spirit,
What is temporal is not what is,

What is eternal is true,
Seek the Father while on the winding paths He leads you,

Do not be dismayed when enemies arise,
when wolves in sheep's clothing are revealed,
It is God shining light within the land field,

Course correct and remove the troll,
although you may pay a toll to pass,
Remember God redeems all prices paid,
on the way to holiness,

Remember you are not prey,
when all is redeemed.
It is not what it seems,

No longer able to hinder,
No longer able to hide,
For the reigning bride's fire from the groom,
exposes the enemy's hind side,

The Bride shall reign with the groom in our hearts, until the triumphant day His presence makes the firmament depart.

PROPHETIC POETRY FOR THE BRIDE

The Bride's Inheritance

It is time for the wheat harvest.
Separation of the wheat and the chaff.

The Holy Spirit removes the chaff with His Ruach.
After the plowing, of the apostolic ones, have broken the former confinements of the former wineskins.
The former wineskins died to expose the wheat for the removal of the chaff.

The Holy Spirit prepares us for the harvest before the Lord.
Ready to be unleavened bread.
A wheat offering for the Lord.

We shall be changed to glorify the Lord.
The corruptible (former wineskin) will be changed to incorruptible (new wineskin)

The blessing for the Bride will be seen amongst the chaff (non-consecrated vessels-five foolish) and the goats (rejected Jesus).

The famine shall not touch those with the oil (Holy Spirit) and the wine (blood covenant) within the new wineskin.

Wealth transfer shall prevail until all the Bride's dowry (inheritance) is complete.
The Bride shall reside in her promised land from the Messiah, her Bridegroom, Jesus.
He will ensure the occupation, citizenship, in Israel and Judah until His return.

While awaiting His return, the Bride does the will of the Father and Son.
Kingdom of God be established in the earth.

We are living scrolls from before time begun.

PROPHETIC POETRY FOR THE BRIDE

The Bride's Oil Revealed

Lord, it is finished,
the oil that was left in the temple from the victory of the Maccabees was not contaminated,
The vial contained consecrated oil,

God has left consecrated oil in the Bride,
The Bride has oil that has not been tampered with,
of their office and gifts in their spirit,

He has protected, hidden this oil so that it was not utilized,
Many of the Bride have not walked fully in their authority
due to God's protection, training, and progression,

The truth is His glory is still within,
He forgives us of all our sins,

We die with Jesus, death to the first Adam,
We arise, resurrect as a new creation,
The second Adam, Jesus.

The veil was removed when Jesus was resurrected,
All veils will be removed from the resurrected remnant,

Like Abraham and others waited in paradise a part of sheol until God
redeemed them through Jesus' resurrection,

Jesus made a spectacle of the enemy,
Took back the keys (authority) of death from him,

Released His remnant to heaven,
The Bride shall see resurrection of God's power in us.
The Bride shall change into who we are in heaven,
Walking on this earth,
Better than the former glory of Israel, walking after redemption, with no feebleness amongst them.
The Bride shall have the latter glory!
Resurrected glory.
We have and will see what it is like to have our sins forgiven.
Like the leper that Jesus said, your sins are forgiven.
Praise God!

MY NOTES

CHAPTER 3

THE MONTH OF SIVAN
MAY-JUN

ENGGAMICKENS.COM

TRIBE OF ZEBULUN

The Tribe of Zebulun Is associated with the month of Sivan.

Sivan is the **ninth month** in the **Jewish Civil Calendar** and the **third month** in the **Jewish Biblical Calendar**.

MONTH'S SIGNIFICANCE

In the month of Sivan, we celebrate the giving of the Torah on the holiday of Shavuot. The Feast of Weeks is a Jewish holiday that occurs on the sixth day of the Hebrew month of Sivan. Wheat Harvest. During Shavuot the Torah was revealed by God to the Israelite nation at Mount Sinai.

PROPHETIC WORD

ZEBULUN TRIBE: MARKETPLACE AND SHIPS/MERCHANTS

BRIDE: PREPARATION FOR THE WHEAT HARVEST SEPARATION

REVELATION

TRIBE OF ZEBULUN'S BLESSINGS

The Patriarch Jacob (Israel's) Blessing

Jacob, the Patriarch after Issac, and Abraham, known as Israel, pronounced a blessing over his 12 sons. Israel's son, Zebulun was the tenth son.

Jacob's Blessing to Zebulun:

Genesis 49:13

13 Zebulun will live by the seashore
and become a haven for ships;
his border will extend toward Sidon.

The Deliverer Moses' Blessing

Zebulun's Blessing:

Moses said this about Zebulun:

Deuteronomy 33:18-19

18 About Zebulun he said:
"Rejoice, Zebulun, in your going out, and you, Issachar, in your tents.

19 They will summon peoples to the mountain and there offer the sacrifices of the righteous; they will feast on the abundance of the seas,
on the treasures hidden in the sand."

PROPHETIC POETRY FOR THE BRIDE

The Calling Out of the Bride

The place in the cave,
was a place of development,
process and training,

I am calling you to your Office,
I am calling you to your Rank,

Know your position,
Take your position,
Serve in it well,

New terrain
Intercessors interceding,
Ascension bound,

Barriers broken,
New words spoken,

Revelation flows,
Like a river,
Living water with pure intensity,

Vision clear,
Ears keen,

Mind resolute,
No longer mute,

No longer small,
Expansion and increase in view,
Breaker has gone forth for you.

MY NOTES

CHAPTER 4

THE MONTH OF TAMMUZ
JUN-JUL

ENGGAMICKENS.COM

TRIBE OF REUBEN

The Tribe of Reuben is associated with the month of Tammuz.

Tammuz is the **tenth month** in the **Jewish Civil Calendar** and the **fourth** month in the **Jewish Biblical Calendar**.

MONTH'S SIGNIFICANCE

This month marks the beginning of the destruction of the Holy Temple in Jerusalem. The 17th day of Tammuz—a fast day that commemorates the day when the walls of Jerusalem were breached by the Romans (in 69 C.E.)—marks the beginning of a period known as "the Three Weeks."

TAMMUZ

PROPHETIC WORD

Repentance
Redemption and Wisdom.

Be discerning with your choices.

Test/Exile
Testimony or Judgement

TRIBE OF REUBEN'S BLESSINGS

The Patriarch Jacob (Israel 's) Blessing

Jacob, the Patriarch after Issac, and Abraham, known as Israel, pronounced a blessing over his **12** sons. Israel's son, Reuben, was his first son.

Jacob's Blessing:

Genesis 49:3

Reuben

3 Reuben, you are my firstborn,
   my might, the first sign of my strength,
   excelling in honor, excelling in power.
4 Turbulent as the waters, you will no longer excel,
   for you went up onto your father's bed,
   onto my couch and defiled it.

The Deliverer Moses' Blessing

Moses led the children of Israel from Egypt. He pronounced a blessing over the tribe of Reuben.

Moses' Blessing:

Deuteronomy 33:6

6 Let Reuben live and not die, nor his people be few.

PROPHETIC POETRY FOR THE BRIDE
Maturation

The Lord says I am exposing the chaff from amongst you.
I have plowed, threshed as the breaker, the wheat to the ground.
And exposed the wheat (Bride) to the sun (Son).

The Holy Spirit consecrated you from what was unholy.
He exposed to separate,

He exposed to annihilate.
The washing begins with consecration fire separating the wheat from the tare.

Sheep from goat.
Holy from unholy.

The separation of the wheat and the chaff.
Inner court, wheat from outer court, chaff.

Cleansing by the Holy Spirit to die to self.
Not I who lives but God (Jesus) that is within me.

Resurrection from the outer court.
New wineskin for the revealing to the world the Sons of the living God.
Manifestation.

PROPHETIC POETRY FOR THE BRIDE

The Bride Be Ready

Be ready to receive,
be ready for His goodness,
The expansion of the Kingdom of God in you,
To have the capacity to fulfill God's will to do works through you,

Rest, no toil,
Selfless, not spoiled,

Consecrated, set apart,
operating in a new wineskin, new start,
New Blend, new life,

Rest not strife,
Victory not defeat,
Never prey, elevated seat,

Promotion for the meek,
We arise from the cave,
as Jesus from the grave,

Isaiah 60 and 61 for all to see,
recompense and reign.
Amos 9:13

PROPHETIC POETRY FOR THE BRIDE

The Bride' Provision

I am opening up wells you dug and I am pouring in.
I am sending the laborers to reap the harvest.

I am sending provision to fund the vision.
Sight is coming, manifestation will be seen.

Your substance will be renown and come from the king.
Glory shall be your portion and fill your vessel.

I see you and you will have what I say.
I decree your portion comes to you without delay.

I loose the kingdom to you and through you this day.
Remember my beloved I am breathing on you afresh in a new way.

My fire you requested will burn bright.
What I put in you will come to the light.

Run with boldness for it will be.
You standing and decreeing as favor rests on thee.

No longer barren, no longer molten.

No longer just manna or just enough.
Overflow is your portion.

You have the right stuff,
No longer prey, to yesterday.

Protected and favored is your portion.
You are beloved lavished in my protection.

Arise and accelerate in what I decreed.
Propel in what I promised thee.
Shine like the dawn.
For your future is bright,
Your table is set
You will see with clear light.

MY NOTES

CHAPTER 5

THE MONTH OF AV
JUL-AUG

ENGGAMICKENS.COM

TRIBE OF SIMEON

The Tribe of Simeon is associated with the month of AV.

AV is the **eleventh month** in the **Jewish Civil Calendar** and the **fifth month** in the **Jewish Biblical Calendar.**

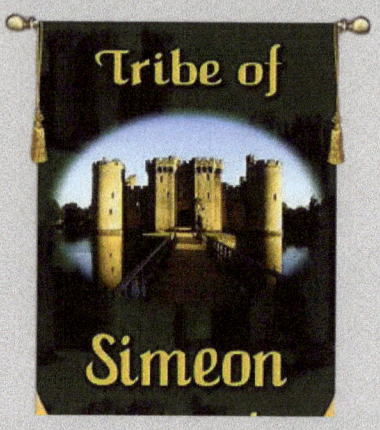

MONTH'S SIGNIFICANCE

In this month, both the first and second Holy Temples were destroyed; we also celebrate 15 Av, a marriage holiday.

PROPHETIC WORD

TRIBE SIMEON: TO LISTEN

THIS AV THE BRIDE IS PREPARING TO RISE WHILE THE FORMER TEMPLE DIES (OLD WINESKIN)

COMFORT IN HIS WILL

TRIBE OF SIMEON'S BLESSINGS

The Patriarch Jacob (Israel 's) Blessing

Jacob, the Patriarch after Issac, and Abraham, known as Israel, pronounced a blessing over his **12** sons. Israel's son, Simeon, was his second son.

Jacob's Blessing:

Gen. 49:5-7

5 Simeon and Levi are brothers—
their swords are weapons of violence.

6 Let me not enter their council,
let me not join their assembly,
for they have killed men in their anger
and hamstrung oxen as they pleased.

7 Cursed be their anger, so fierce,
and their fury, so cruel!
I will scatter them in Jacob and disperse them in Israel.

The Deliverer Moses' Blessing

Moses led the children of Israel from Egypt. He pronounced a blessing over the tribe of Simeon.

Moses Blessing: None

Joshua 19:1

1 Moses has no blessing for Simeon in this chapter, because the tribe of Simeon largely merged with Judah and came under Judah's covering. Thus, the blessing of Judah also applied to Simeon.

PROPHETIC POETRY FOR THE BRIDE

The Bride Goes Through the Straits

Bride as we go through the straits, we must possess the gates.
As we use our light to see the way, we must remember we carry the day,
Your swords, your decrees, remove roots as well as trees,

What was not planted by the Father, we must remove.
Reproof, correction, with strokes we move,
Use your shield against the lies and deception,
Let the Holy Spirit, the Spirit of Truth be our weapon.

Rebuild, rebuild the ruined places takes time,
As we are plowing, God is renewing the wine.
Oil from the Father will cause our fire to burn bright.
Turning night to day in our sight.

It is not barren for what you plowed has seed.
It doesn't look plentiful due to it is devoid of the weeds,
Tare removed and chaff threshed.
Chaff crushed, winnowing fork will take it away.
As the Spirit of the Lord, blows away the decay.

The Father waters, the Holy Spirit germinates.
The consummation takes place.
Fire from above saturates the alter ablaze, oil in our lamps.

We are a lampstand which holds His oil.
We are a lampstand which possesses His fire.
We carry the light of God for the world to see.
We stand strong, those who choose to go with us will possess his light.
For those will be given the gift of sight

Revelation will be their portion.
Transformation will be their manifestation.
To be a container, a vessel, shaped for its use.

MY NOTES

CHAPTER 6

THE MONTH OF ELUL
AUG-SEPT

ENGGAMICKENS.COM

TRIBE OF GAD

The Tribe of GAD is associated with the month of ELUL.

Kislev is the twelfth month in the Jewish Civil Calendar and the sixth month in the Jewish Biblical Calendar.

MONTH'S SIGNIFICANCE

It is called "the month of repentance," "the month of mercy" and "the month of forgiveness."

PROPHETIC WORD

GAD TRIBE OF WAR. MEN OF WAR, FACES OF LIONS, ENLARGE TERRITORY

REPENT AND LET GO OF THE OLD WINESKIN AND TARES, FINISH BUILDING THE WALLS OF THE TEMPLE,

KING IS IN THE FIELD ABOUND AND OVERFLOW

TRIBE OF GAD'S BLESSINGS

The Patriarch Jacob (Israel's) Blessing

Jacob, the Patriarch after Issac, and Abraham, known as Israel, pronounced a blessing over his **12** sons. Israel's son, Gad, was his seventh son.

Jacob's Blessing:

Gen. 49:19

19 will be attacked by a band of raiders,
   but he will attack them at their heels.

The Deliverer Moses' Blessing

Moses led the children of Israel from Egypt. He pronounced a blessing over the tribe of Gad.

Moses' Blessing:

Deuteronomy 33:20-21

20 About Gad he said: "Blessed is he who enlarges Gad's domain! Gad lives there like a lion, tearing at arm or head.

21 He chose the best land for himself; the leader's portion was kept for him. When the heads of the people assembled, he carried out the Lord's righteous will, and his judgments concerning Israel.

PROPHETIC POETRY FOR THE BRIDE
The Bride Old Wineskin Transforming into the New

Mind shift, birth,
Mind shift, remove the curse,

Mind shift, move pass the decrees,
Mind shift, into who I am supposed to be,

Mind shift, from complacent to fire,
Mind shift, from waiting for the glory,

To manifesting God's desire and fire,
Mind shift, from who I want to be,
into maturity,

Mind shift, from Lo-Debar to the palace,
Mind shift, from servant to son,

Mind shift, to seeing God's handiwork being done,
Mind shift, from what was to what is,

Mind shift, to beloved to His.

MY NOTES

CHAPTER 7

THE MONTH OF TISHERI SEPT-OCT

ENGGAMICKENS.COM

TRIBE OF EPHRAIM

The Tribe of Ephraim is associated with the month.

Tisheri is the first month in the Jewish Civil Calendar and the seventh month in the Jewish Biblical Calendar.

MONTH'S SIGNIFICANCE

TISHREI (TISHRI), THE FIRST MONTH OF THE JEWISH YEAR (THE SEVENTH WHEN COUNTING FROM NISAN), IS FULL OF MOMENTOUS AND MEANINGFUL DAYS OF CELEBRATION. BEGINNING WITH THE HIGH HOLIDAYS, IN THIS MONTH WE CELEBRATE ROSH HASHANA.

TISHREI IS CONSIDERED THE "HEAD" OF THE YEAR, AND THE RESERVOIR FROM WHICH WE DRAW OUR STRENGTH AND INSPIRATION THROUGHOUT THE YEAR AHEAD.

PROPHETIC WORD

EPHRAIM WAS BLESSED TO BE FRUITFUL

TISHERI
HEAD OF THE YEAR!
REFER TO THE DECADE OF PEY 80 (THE MOUTH: DECREE).

RETRIBUTION & JUDGEMENT
JOY OR PUNISHMENT

TRIBE OF EPHRAIM'S BLESSINGS

The Patriarch Jacob (Israel's) Blessing

Jacob, the Patriarch after Issac, and Abraham, known as Israel, pronounced a blessing over his 12 sons. Israel's son Joseph was his eleventh son. Joseph had two sons who inherited land and blessings. One of which is called Ephraim.

Jacob's Blessing - Gen. 48:19-20
"...However, his younger brother shall be greater than he, and his descendants shall become a multitude of nations. And he blessed them that day, saying, 'By you Israel shall pronounce blessing, saying, 'May God make you like Ephraim and Manasseh!' Thus he put Ephraim before Manasseh."

The Deliverer Moses' Blessing

Moses led the children of Israel from Egypt. He pronounced a blessing over the tribe of Ephraim.

Moses' Blessing:

Deuteronomy 33:13-17

13 About Joseph he said:
"May the Lord bless his land with the precious dew from heaven above
 and with the deep waters that lie below;

14 with the best the sun brings forth and the finest the moon can yield;

15 with the choicest gifts of the ancient mountains and the fruitfulness of the everlasting hills;

16 with the best gifts of the earth and its fullness and the favor of him who dwelt in the burning bush. Let all these rest on the head of Joseph, on the brow of the prince among[e] his brothers.

17 In majesty he is like a firstborn bull; is horns are the horns of a wild ox.
With them he will gore the nations, even those at the ends of the earth.
Such are the ten thousands of Ephraim; such are the thousands of Manasseh."

PROPHETIC POETRY FOR THE BRIDE
The Bride Awaits

How many tears?
How many words unfulfilled?
How long does the enemy have until my Bridegroom, the Breaker,
breaks the bars of iron,
the gates of brass,
How long do we cry out?
How long does this last,
Words, decrees,
Breathe resurrecting life unto these,
Bareness, baldness
to fruitfulness and beauty.
Ashes I given,
tears sown,
Waiting on thee,
The love that I've known,
Your hand can reach me,
Your love can consume me,
Oh, how I yearn for intimacy,
Breathe life into me,
Resurrect what has died due to the enemy's hand,
Consecrate me with holiness,
so, I can have a clean heart and pure hands,
Each day, each week, each month, and each year has gone by,
I war to hold on to God's word,
I ask for life to move forward,
Encourage myself and others,
as we move to our calling,
Awaiting our reward,
though You tarry, I wait,
As I look and decree another day,
Waiting for God's word to be fulfilled and manifest this day

MY NOTES

CHAPTER 8

THE MONTH OF CHESVAN
OCT-NOV

ENGGAMICKENS.COM

TRIBE OF MANASSEH

The Tribe of Manasseh is associated with the month of Cheshvan.

Chesvan is the **second month** in the **Jewish Civil Calendar** and the **eighth month** in the **Jewish Biblical Calendar**.

MONTH'S SIGNIFICANCE

MarCheshvan (sometimes called Cheshvan) is the second month of the Jewish calendar counting from Rosh Hashanah (the eighth from Nisan). Cheshvan is the only month that does not have any holidays or special mitzvot.

CHESVAN

PROPHETIC WORD

TRIBE OF MANASSEH

GOD WILL CAUSE US TO FORGET THE CHAFF

NEW BEGINNINGS

TRIBE OF MANASSEH'S BLESSINGS

The Patriarch Jacob (Israel's) Blessing

Jacob, the Patriarch after Issac, and Abraham, known as Israel, pronounced a blessing over his 12 sons. Israel's son, Joseph, was his eleventh son. Joseph had two sons who inherited land and blessings. One of which is called Manasseh.

Jacob's Blessing:

Gen. 48:19-20

19 But his father refused and said, "I know, my son, I know. He too will become a people, and he too will become great. Nevertheless, his younger brother will be greater than he, and his descendants will become a group of nations."

20 He blessed them that day and said,
"In your name will Israel pronounce this blessing:
May God make you like Ephraim and Manasseh.
So, he put Ephraim ahead of Manasseh."

The Deliverer Moses' Blessing

Moses led the children of Israel from Egypt. He pronounced Joseph's blessing over the tribe of Manasseh.

Moses' Blessing:

Deuteronomy 33:13-17

13 About Joseph he said:
"May the Lord bless his land
with the precious dew from heaven above
and with the deep waters that lie below;

14 with the best the sun brings forth
and the finest the moon can yield;

15 with the choicest gifts of the ancient mountains
and the fruitfulness of the everlasting hills;

16 with the best gifts of the earth and its fullness
and the favor of him who dwelt in the burning bush.
Let all these rest on the head of Joseph,
on the brow of the prince among his brothers.

17 In majesty he is like a firstborn bull;
his horns are the horns of a wild ox.
With them he will gore the nations,
even those at the ends of the earth.
Such are the ten thousands of Ephraim;
such are the thousands of Manasseh."

PROPHETIC POETRY FOR THE BRIDE

The Bride Arises

Oh, the Lord speaks,
He guides, He reminds me of His promises,
Oh, the release the oil, the new wine,
the new wineskin,
consecration God sanctification in you,

No more molten feathers,
No more torn beaks,
No more wanting onions and leeks,
Taste and see,

Promises manifest miracles in plain sight,
Oh, Jerusalem and Judah delights,
the Bride dances like Miriam,

Glory no longer concealed,
Glory of the son revealed,

Oxen and eagles convergence emerge from out of the caves,
Glory and power surge for all to see,

Advance is His charge,
Take dominion with glee,

As God pours out His goodness,
Like Him, we reign,

Angels go forth,
once again.

PROPHETIC POETRY FOR THE BRIDE

Oneness

As Jesus arises in His Bride,
all will see,
the glory that was hidden arise in thee.

Oh, how glorious,
Oh, what splendor.

Being one with our Bridegroom,
complete surrender.

Change in spirit,
Change in soul,
Change in Appearance.

Like the Book of Acts,
scenes to behold.

We waited,
We trimmed our wicks.
Pursued more oil,
We kept moving forward, removing the soil.

Access granted, garments changed.
Wise virgin to the Bride of Christ.

The ultimate exchange!

MY NOTES

CHAPTER 9

THE MONTH OF KISLEV
NOV-DEC

TRIBE OF BENJAMIN

The Tribe of Benjamin is associated with the month Kislev.

Kislev is the **third month** in the **Jewish Civil Calendar** and the **ninth month** in the **Jewish Biblical calendar**.

MONTH'S SIGNIFICANCE

Kislev is best known for the holiday of Chanukah (Hannukah) and the New Year.

KISLEV

PROPHETIC WORD

BIRTHING FOR THE HARVEST

TRIBE OF BENJAMIN'S BLESSINGS

The Patriarch Jacob (Israel's) Blessing

Jacob, the Patriarch after Issac, and Abraham, known as Israel, pronounced a blessing over his **12** sons. Israel's son, Benjamin, was his twelfth son.

Jacob's Blessing

Genesis 49:27

27 Benjamin, is a predatory wolf; in the morning he will devour prey and in the evening he will distribute spoils.

The Deliverer Moses' Blessing

Moses led the children of Israel from Egypt. He pronounced a blessing over the tribe of Benjamin.

Moses' Blessing:

Deuteronomy 33:12

12 About Benjamin he said:
"Let the beloved of the Lord rest secure in him, for he shields him all day long, and the one the Lord loves rests between his shoulders."

PROPHETIC POETRY FOR THE BRIDE
The Bride Price

To let go, what does it mean?
To refrain from pain, how quaint it seems.

To depend on God's vastness, and let go of today,
To say I love you Lord, and yet obey.

To shed, refine, molt away,
to say goodbye to Babylon, is the price we pay.

To be free, and say I wait on thee,
To missed deadlines, due dates, to cause consequence.
To say goodbye, to such offense.

Father, to fly high above the refrain,
To say goodbye to the offense and disdain.

403 years we look to thee,
Who has sent the Breaker to rescue me.

Although my hearts cry on ink bled through,
You kept every thought of what I went through.

To soar, which is my destiny,
To rely on kingdom as the Son removes all mutiny.

An eagle's journey is to hear and see what the Fathers says
And move in obedience to fulfill our destiny within our days.

Saying goodbye to thoughts of an eaglet,
Soaring to greater heights,
As our identity in Christ comes to the light.

We lead, we soar, we fight, and we war,
Heavens host of angels guide, protects, and assists,
As KING Jesus, El Gibhor, El Sabaoth, stands an instructs in our mists.

Kingdom of God reigns, is our goal
To fulfill the will of the Father to behold

PROPHETIC POETRY FOR THE BRIDE
Church or Bride?

Lead us not to go astray,
Hold onto our faith, we pray,

We ask for the Spirit of Faith,
to make it through,
We ask for The Spirit of Truth,
So, deception or delusion will not rule over you,

Lord cleanse us and fill us,
Make Ezekiel 36:25-27, be our portion
To fulfill your decrees and your laws,
To make the enemy of our souls pause,

Some of you don't believe we are in the last days?
Take a look at your ways.

Are you growing cold of the things of God?
Don't become an apostate, and leave the faith.

As the world is full of busyness,
The enemy dulls the senses of what is true,
Makes you feel, God will accept all that you do.

You will see the difference between the sheep and goat,
Don't be a sheep who loses your pure coat (garment)

Sheep must hear God's voice,
To know you are not an apostate of course.

PROPHETIC POETRY FOR THE BRIDE
Which Role will you Play?

Stay firm my bride, for temptation is near,
Do not listen to what tickles the ear,

Remember the 10 virgins, due to this is true,
Who did the 5 foolish listened to?
Paul said who bewitched you?
The doctrine of ease, was said to you,

You do not have to die to self to serve the Lord,
Just take the broad paths of our landlord,

Narrow is the way,
Consecrate to yield to the Holy Spirt today!

Ask to be filled with the Holy Spirit and baptized by the Holy Fire,
To be wise and not led astray, cold as ice, following your desires,
Let no one put out your holy fire,

I will keep those who repent to me, to keep their garments white,
Only my fire, can help you win the fight,
Those who ask me for My heart in them, will I delight,

Church, Bride of Christ, we are in the last days,
The bible is being fulfilled, which role will you agree to play?

PROPHETIC POETRY FOR THE BRIDE
The Bride's Fire

Blessed are they that the Lord has predestined to be written in the Lamb's Book of Life.
The Lord says, we are days away for His promises of washing, redemption, and sonship to be complete. Resurrection power of the Glory to be made manifest in the earth.
Promises fulfilled and purposes revealed.

Oh remnant, oh how you will shine. Oh bride, divine.
I go before you to make the crooked pathways straight,
I, the King of Glory, comes through the gates,
Make ready for my checkmate.

Thou I tarry, do not dismay,
For your hearts shall be filled with joy, I say,

Not of this world, are my sons and daughters,
Your spirit, where I reside,
In the Holy of Holies, no enemy can hide,

Your soul, is being made clean,
The Fuller's soap, reigns supreme,

Iniquities will vanish when I am through,
No longer spots, blemishes and wrinkles to haunt you,

Blameless you shall be before my eyes,
No longer will my courtroom, hear lies,

Blameless are my sheep, for this Shepherd is true,
Oh, how I truly love and adore you,

Make ready, for the feast you are about to partake,
For you will reign through me on this earth for my Father's sake,

Kingdom and purity is my heart's desire,
As I place, in you, my heart and Holy Fire!

MY NOTES

CHAPTER 10

THE MONTH OF TEVET
DEC-JAN

ENGGAMICKENS.COM

TRIBE OF DAN

The Tribe of Dan is associated with the month Tevet.

Tevet is the **fourth** month in the **Jewish Civil Calendar** and the tenth month in the **Jewish Biblical Calendar**.

MONTH'S SIGNIFICANCE

This month begins with the last days of Chanukah (Hannukah).

Esther was summoned by King Xerxes.

Esther became queen to King Xerxes after year of preparation of being bathed in water (symbolic of the Word of God) and oil (symbolic of the Holy Spirit).

PROPHETIC WORD
TENTH MONTH JUDGEMENT OR TESTIMONY"

GOD IS JUDGING

TEST

IF YOU PASS,
IT IS A TESTIMONY,
VICTORY

REMNANT BRIDE IS ADORNED

TRIBE OF DAN'S BLESSINGS

The Patriarch Jacob (Israel's) Blessing

Jacob, the Patriarch after Issac, and Abraham, known as Israel, pronounced a blessing over his **12** sons. Israel's son, Dan, was his fifth son.

Jacob's Blessing:

Genesis 49:16-18

Dan will avenge his people, the tribes of Israel will be united as one. Dan will be a serpent on the highway, a viper by the path, that bites a horse's heels so its rider falls backward. For Your salvation do I long, O Hashem!

The Deliverer Moses' Blessing

Moses led the children of Israel from Egypt. He pronounced a blessing over the tribe of Dan.

Deuteronomy 33:22

22 About Dan he said:
"Dan is a lion's cub, springing out of Bashan."

PROPHETIC POETRY FOR THE BRIDE

Bride's Resurrection Journey!

The Bride arises to build,
Slumber is gone,
Like time that stood still,
Time to crossover,
Time to move in formation,
Time to rebuild for God's nation,
Oil drops from on high,
Fire lights the sacrifice,
Sanctification,
Fresh fire ablaze,
God lights our path to what once was a maze,
The Holy Remnant resurrected from death,
Old wineskins dried out was all that was left,
Fresh wine and fresh oil is our portion and His delight,
His Bride resurrected and moves through the night,
Build, build, is the decree,
While El Sabaoth and His army goes ahead and prepares the way for thee,
The Bridegroom will not be denied
His Bride will be fully adorned,
Oh Bride, resurrect,
The journey has been hard,
I resuscitate what died in its innocence,
I preserve the alpha,
the seed I impregnated you with before you arrived,
Holy Fire, pure in spirit, draws you forth,
From your Father of lights,
As I roar over you,
shakings and decrees,
come into alignment,
plumblines are established,
tribes come together,
with skillsets, anointings, and decrees,
Like sinews,
What will be is,
What is will be,
As it is in heaven,
so will it be on the earth,
Decree, my children and see,
my handiwork of all that I promised thee!

MY NOTES

CHAPTER 11

THE MONTH OF SHEVAT
JAN-FEB

ENGGAMICKENS.COM

TRIBE OF ASHER

11

The Tribe of Asher is associated with the month Shevat.

Shevat is the **fifth month** in the Jewish Civil Calendar and the **eleventh** month in the **Jewish Biblical calendar**.

MONTH'S SIGNIFICANCE

The high point of the month is Tu B'Shevat—the New Year for trees.

SHEVAT

P

PROPHETIC WORD

THE TREES OF RIGHTEOUSNES SHALL BEAR FRUIT

THE WISE REMNANT VIRGINS WILL BE KNOWN

THE HARVEST SHALL APPEAR

TRIBE OF ASHER'S BLESSINGS

The Patriarch Jacob (Israel's) Blessing

Jacob, the Patriarch after Issac, and Abraham, known as Israel, pronounced a blessing over his **12** sons. Israel's son, Asher, was his eighth son.

Jacob's Blessing:

Genesis 49:20

Asher

20 "Asher's food will be rich;
he will provide delicacies fit for a king.

The Deliverer Moses' Blessing

Moses led the children of Israel from Egypt. He pronounced a blessing over the tribe of Asher.

Moses' Blessing:

Deuteronomy 33:24-29

24 About Asher he said: "Most blessed of sons is Asher; let him be favored by his brothers, and let him bathe his feet in oil.

25 The bolts of your gates will be iron and bronze, and your strength will equal your days.

26 'There is no one like the God of Jeshurun, who rides across the heavens to help you and on the clouds in his majesty.

27 The eternal God is your refuge, and underneath are the everlasting arms. He will drive out your enemies before you, saying, 'Destroy them!'

28 So Israel will live in safety; Jacob will dwell secure in a land of grain and new wine, where the heavens drop dew.

29 Blessed are you, Israel! Who is like you, a people saved by the Lord?
He is your shield and helper and your glorious sword. Your enemies will cower before you, and you will tread on their heights."

PROPHETIC POETRY FOR THE BRIDE
The Church Consecrates to Become the Bride

Awake oh church and become the Bride,
The Bride will go in,
The church will remain,

We must transition from the church age to the Kingdom age,
We must ascend from the church to the Bride,
Intimacy with oil produced,
Grapes and olives crushed,
Vintage will appear,
King and Priests with power, posterity, prosperity, and health will arise

The church will arise from her slumber,
make the choice to become the Bride,
and carry the oil of salvation, righteousness, and purity,
Or become foolish,
not discerning the time of harvest,

The last shall become first,
blessed are those who come in the last hour,
for they shall be filled,

Do not forsake your time of visitation,
Lord bless us to walk in obedience syncopated with you,

Let us receive at our times of visitation.
The Head of the Year,

New Year, coronation,
Summer to remember, you.

PROPHETIC POETRY FOR THE BRIDE

The Ruach

As the wind blows,
our destinies become clear,

As the Ruach of God clears the path,
Stand clear of the aftermath,

Judge rightly, discern well,
See with spiritual sight from your kingdom reign,

Decree, Sons of God decree,
Laws are established for thee,

King and Priest, rule from above,
earthly insight is not an aerial view,

Eagle eyes is what I gave you,
foresight, detail, intel,
mysteries revealed, glory unconcealed,

Flames of fire, burn bright,
Light up the night,

Zerubbabel and Joshua become one like I, Jesus, in you,
like the Father and the Son,

The Bride's posterity manifests.
As the five foolish, watch and see,
the feast table I prepared for thee,

King of Kings be glorified,
as your Brides come into their fullness which they can no longer hide.

PROPHETIC POETRY FOR THE BRIDE
The Bride Will Ascend

Wheat from tare distinction,
Chaff, old wineskin,
Wheat, new wineskin, gold, glory, revelation, power, wisdom, prosperity, and posterity,
Quick elevation to match your spiritual revelation,
Thy Kingdom come,

Wheat transformed,
Outer garment removed,
New garment revealed,

New man, new creation revealed,
Prepared for the harvest,
The fullness of the gentiles, reveal the King of Glory,
To reap with the sickle into the wedding feast,

God is giving us our new wine which is a covenant contract,

His glory, wine is shared as a seal to our covenant betrothal.
The Bride focused on our purity, wedding to the Lamb of God, our garments,
and asking for the filling of the Holy Spirit,

The Bride is betrothed, married,
awaiting the date of His return,

Contract before God and His blessings of love from the Bridegroom,
His blessings of wealth is coming soon,

Elevation of status coming from Father's home into the Bridegroom's Huppah,
You were betrothed when you gave me your heart & became born again,

When the Holy Spirit filled you,
He brought you to me and you were purified then,
Since then, you needed more cleansing,
therefore, the Holy Spirit consecrated you back to me,
and is preparing you for me to meet me in the Huppah,
You are baptized afresh with fire, cleansed ready for me,
I am in the Huppah to pour out new wine again with intimacy,
Consummated you will be, for my glory to be as one for all to see

MY NOTES

MY NOTES

CHAPTER 12

THE MONTH OF ADAR
FEB-MAR

ENGGAMICKENS.COM

TRIBE OF NAPHTALI

The Tribe of Naphtali is associated with the month Adar.
Adar is the **sixth month** in the **Jewish Civil Calendar** and the twelfth month in the **Jewish Biblical Calendar**.

MONTH'S SIGNIFICANCE

The spirit of Purim is in the entire month, making it a time of rejoicing and good mazal (fortune) for the Jewish people.

ADAR

PROPHETIC WORD

WE WILL TRANSFORM LIKE ESTHER AND TAKE OUR POSITION

DECREES IN OUR FAVOR

TRIBE OF NAPHTALI'S BLESSINGS

The Patriarchs and Deliverer's Blessing

The Patriarch Jacob (Israel's) Blessing

Jacob, the Patriarch after Issac, and Abraham, known as Israel, pronounced a blessing over his 12 sons. Israel's son, Naphatli, was his sixth son.

Jacob's Blessing:

Genesis 49:21

"Naphtali

21 "Naphtali is a doe set free
   that bears beautiful fawns.

The Deliverer Moses' Blessing

Moses led the children of Israel from Egypt. He pronounced a blessing over the tribe of Naphtali.

Moses' Blessing:

Deuteronomy 33:23

23 About Naphtali he said:
"Naphtali is abounding with the favor of the Lord
  and is full of his blessing; he will inherit southward to the lake."

PROPHETIC POETRY FOR THE BRIDE
Bridegroom, The Five Wise and Five Foolish

The Bride is summoned to the Huppah, the chambers of the Bridegroom,
Protection, intimacy, and honor,
We which contend for more oil.
Seek Him, in the field,
I am my beloved and He is mine,

He is reminding me of the ten virgins,
Testing.
When they awoke from their slumber,
some consecrated (the five wise),
and some did not (the five foolish),
When the ten virgins heard the beaconing,
they arose to meet the King (bridegroom) in the field,

When times got dark, hard, and difficult,
the five foolish realized the five wise had oil,
peace, favor, power, and prosperity,

The five foolish asked the five wise for what they had,
the five wise said go and get yours,
we have enough for ourselves to make it to the king, our bridegroom,

Consecrate yourselves and seek the Holy Spirit the giver (exchanger) of the oil,
The five foolish then turned back to seek the oil.
some repented and some did not,

Currently, the five foolish have time,
while the harvest is ripe until the fullness of the gentiles,
The time is shortening,
The season is growing dark,
Those who carry the light will warn others to turn to the Lord while the Holy Spirit can be found,

There is a time until the door is shut,
We will ascend to the Most High God with our Bridegroom Jesus

PROPHETIC POETRY FOR THE BRIDE

The Bride and the Alter

As I lay things on the alter,
to test what is true,

For God to judge and not mine eye,
For God's discernment in a matter,

To bring peace to His will,
on matters to be still,

While we wait to see,
What His verdict may be,

I recall the words shouting forth from my destiny,
align, alignment, plumbline,

Only what is pure,
remains on the vine,

From ashes we exchange what has died for beauty,
from what is left from the pruning,

Is the remnant to begin again,
to charge to go forth,
heaven, Kingdom of God, true north,

East gate from whenst we enter and exit,
The East wind judges and brings justice to God's will,
peace be still.

MY NOTES

Call to Repentance, Salvation, and Fresh Fire

If, after reading this book of prophetic and poetic psalms, you find yourself thinking am I lukewarm? Have I experienced a consecration with God since 2020? If you are questioning if you are a part of the Bride of Christ or whether it cost to follow Jesus? If you are thinking, I haven't asked the Holy Spirit if it is His will for me to do this or that. Have I grown spiritually? Is my wineskin, vessel, or temple, feeling dry from the lack of intimacy with the Holy Spirit?

Ask Him to forgive you of every transgression, idolatry, iniquity, soul tie, demonic agreement, demonic covenant, demonic spirit spouse, and demonic altar. You must speak this to the Lord from your heart. If you have problems stating these words, ask God to help you. Ask God to send the Holy Spirit to place fresh fire upon you to burn up everything that is not like Him and to baptize you with His Spirit. Ask God for the Spirit of the Lord, Spirit of Wisdom, Spirit of Knowledge, Spirit of Understanding, Spirit of Fear of the Lord, Spirit of Might, and Spirit of Counsel. Isaiah 11:2-3.

If you ask God to forgive and baptize you with fresh Holy Fire, watch God separate the tares from you (people and things that are not of Him) and remove the chaff (old mindsets of self-sufficiency without seeking God) from you. God's word state those who suffer with Hiim shall reign with Him. You will be positioned for a new wineskin for the Lord to fill with His glory. In the Book of Revelation, the upcoming famine will not have permission to touch those with the new wineskin, which contains the new oil (anointing from the Holy Spirit) and new wine (new covenant of Jesus blood which was shed for you).

If you prayed this prayer aloud, God heard you and will prepare you for the harvest as true wheat. Welcome to the Bride of Christ. Email me at info@enggamickens.com if this book led you into deeper intimacy with the Father. For those who are on fire, fresh fire is always good for the spirit, soul, and body.

Glossary of Terms

Bride of Christ: The bride of Christ or the lamb's wife is a term used in reference to a group of related verses in the Bible, in the Gospels, Revelation, the Epistles and related verses in the Old Testament. Sometimes, the bride is implied by calling Jesus a bridegroom. For over 1500 years, the Church was identified as the bride betrothed to Christ. However, there are instances of the interpretation of the usage varying from church to church. Most believe that it always refers to the church. -Wikipedia

Church: Church is this text is referred to as ten virgins who woke up to hear the sound of the Bridegroom Jesus. The five foolish virgins did not think they needed to consecrate to receive more oil (anointing) from Holy Spirit vs. the Bride of Christ/Ekklesia are like the five wise virgins who continually communed with the Holy Spirit for more oil (anointing) until to have light to last until they met the bridegroom. See Matthew 25:1-13.
The Greek word ekklēsia, literally "called out" or "called forth" and commonly used to indicate a group of individuals called to gather for some function, in particular an assembly of the citizens of a city, as in Acts 19:32–41, is the New Testament term referring to the Christian Church (either a particular local congregation or the whole body of the faithful). -Wikipedia

El Sabaoth: Tzevaot, Tsebaoth or Sabaoth (צבאות, ṣəḇāʾōṯ, [tsvaot] (listen), lit. "Armies"), usually translated "Hosts", appears in reference to armies or armed hosts of men but is not used as a divine epithet in the Torah, Joshua, or Judges. Starting in the Books of Samuel, the term "Lord of Hosts" appears hundreds of times throughout the Prophetic books, in Psalms, and in Chronicles. -Wikipedia

Glossary of Terms

Exile/Judgement (Three weeks of sorrow): The children of Israel went through four exiles due to disobedience to God. he Three Weeks is an annual mourning period that falls out in the summer. This is when we mourn the destruction of the Holy Temple and our launch into a still-ongoing exile. The period begins on the 17th of the Hebrew month of Tammuz, a fast day that marks the day when the walls of Jerusalem were breached by the Romans in 69 CE. It reaches its climax and concludes with the fast of the 9th of Av, the date when both Holy Temples were set aflame. This is the saddest day of the Jewish calendar, and it is also the date that many other tragedies befell our people. -Chabad.org

Exodus: The Exodus (Hebrew: יציאת מצרים, Yeẕi'at Miẕrayim: lit. 'Departure from Egypt') is the founding myth of the Israelites whose narrative is spread over four books of the Torah or Pentateuch, namely Exodus, Leviticus, Numbers, and Deuteronomy. -Wikipedia
Forty days of Teshuvah: The Forty Days of Teshuvah represent the second forty days that Moses spent on Mount Sinai after the Golden Calf idolatry. The first thirty days ending on Yom Teruah is generally known as the Time of Repentance.

Feast of Weeks: Shavuot ("Weeks"), commonly known in English as the Feast of Weeks, is a Jewish holiday that occurs on the sixth day of the Hebrew month of Sivan (in the 21st century, it may fall between May 15 and June 14 on the Gregorian calendar). In the Bible, Shavuot marked the wheat harvest in the Land of Israel (Exodus 34:22). In addition, Orthodox rabbinic traditions teach that the date also marks the revelation of the Torah to Moses and the Israelites at Mount Sinai, which, according to the tradition of Orthodox Judaism, occurred at this date in 1314 BCE.[2]-Wikipedia

Five foolish virgins: See Church.

Five wise virgins: See Bride of Christ and reference to the Bride of Christ in the glossary term Church.

Glossary of Terms

Fuller's soap: FULLER's SOAP, Heb. phrase, וּכְבֹרִית מְכַבְּסִים, consisting of a term בְּרִית, H1383, "alkaline salt," "natural lye" extracted from the Asiatic soap plants such as Mesembrianthemum cristallinum; Salicornia solacea; Salsala kali and the like (cf. I. Löw, Die Flora der Juden [1924-1934]) which are reduced by burning to produce a pasty mass used as a bleach, esp. in the presence of olive oil. The other term is the common Sem. term כָּבַס, H3891, "to tread," "knead" and thus to wash in the Near Eastern fashion. - www.biblegateway.com

In Malachi 3:2-3 the day of the Lord's coming is said to be "like a refiner's fire and like fullers' soap (to cleanse)."

Goat: The goat is a reprobate or those who deny the son of God, Holy Spirit, or God.

Hanukkah/Chanuka/Hanuhah: Hanukkah[a] (/ˈhɑːnəkə/; Hebrew: חֲנֻכָּה, Modern: Ḥanuka, Tiberian: Ḥanukā listen), also known as the Festival of Lights (Hebrew: חַג הָאוּרִים, Ḥag HaUrim), is a Jewish festival commemorating the recovery of Jerusalem and subsequent rededication of the Second Temple at the beginning of the Maccabean revolt against the Seleucid Empire in the 2nd century BCE. -Wikipedia

Huppah: A chuppah (Hebrew: חוּפָּה, pl. חוּפּוֹת, chuppot, literally, "canopy" or "covering"), also huppah, chipe, chupah, or chuppa, is a canopy under which a Jewish couple stand during their wedding ceremony. It consists of a cloth or sheet, sometimes a tallit, stretched or supported over four poles, or sometimes manually held up by attendants to the ceremony. A chuppah symbolizes the home that the couple will build together. - Wikipedia

Lo-Debar: Lo-debar (Hebrew: לא דבר, romanized: Lōḏəḇār) was a town in the Old Testament in Gilead not far from Mahanaim, north of the Jabbok river (2 Samuel 9:4–5)[1] in ancient Israel. It is mentioned in the Hebrew Bible as the home of Machir, a contemporary of David. (2 Samuel 9:4,5). -Wikipedia

Glossary of Terms

Omer Count: Counting of the Omer (Hebrew: סְפִירַת הָעוֹמֶר, Sefirat HaOmer, sometimes abbreviated as Sefira or the Omer) is an important verbal counting of each of the forty-nine days starting with the Wave Offering of a sheaf of ripe grain with a sacrifice immediately following the commencement (Hebrew: רֵאשִׁית, reishit) of the grain harvest, and the First Fruits festival celebrating the end of the grain harvest, known as Feast of Weeks/Shavuot/Pentecost in Mosaic Law (Hebrew Bible: Deuteronomy 16:9-12, Leviticus 23:10-16); or in the varying current Jewish holidays traditions, the period between the Passover or Feast of Unleavened Bread, and Shavuot. This is the second of the three annual Mosaic Law feast periods. - Wikipedia

Passover: Passover, also called Pesach (/ˈpɛsɑːx, ˈpeɪ-/;[2] Biblical Hebrew: חַג הַפֶּסַח, romanized: Ḥag haPesaḥ), is a major Jewish holiday that celebrates the exodus of the Israelites from slavery in Egypt,[3] which occurs on the 15th day of the Hebrew month of Nisan, the first month of Aviv, or spring. The word Pesach or Passover can also refer to the Korban Pesach, the paschal lamb that was offered when the Temple in Jerusalem stood; to the Passover Seder, the ritual meal on Passover night; or to the Feast of Unleavened Bread. -Wikipedia

Purim: Purim (/ˈpʊərɪm/; Hebrew: פּוּרִים Pūrīm, lit. 'lots'; see Name below) is a Jewish holiday which commemorates the saving of the Jewish people from Haman, an official of the Achaemenid Empire who was planning to have all of Persia's Jewish subjects killed, as recounted in the Book of Esther (usually dated to the 5th century BCE). -Wikipedia

Remnant: The Bride of Christ who will be raptured. There are also remnants within the remnant meaning there are those who are of the Bride of Christ who will be given apostolic anointing to help bring in the harvest (the rest of the Bride of Christ). According to the Book of Isaiah, the "remnant" (Hebrew: שְׁאָר, romanized:sh'ár) is a small group of Israelites who will survive the invasion of the Assyrian army under Tiglath-Pileser III (Isaiah10:20-22).

Ruach: Rûach (רוּחַ) has the meanings "wind, spirit, breath," and elohim can mean "great" as well as "god".- Wikipedia

Glossary of Terms

Sabbath: The Sabbath is a weekly day of rest or time of worship given in the Bible as the seventh day. -Wikipedia

Sabbath Year or Shmita: (Hebrew: שמטה, Shemittah, literally "release"), is the seventh (שביעי, shebiy'iy) year of the seven-year agricultural cycle mandated by Torah for the Land of Israel, relatively little observed in biblical tradition, but still observed in contemporary Judaism.-Wikipedia

(4) Sabbaths: The Four Sabbaths before Passover. Collectively, these four Sabbaths are called "The Four Shabbatot" and additional Torah readings (Arba Parashiyot - four Torah portions) are read that connect with the two holidays. The names of these Sabbaths are Shabbat Shekalim, Shabbat Zakhor, Shabbat Parah, and Shabbat HaChodesh. -Hebrews4Christians.com

Season of Joy: Season of Our Joy is a 'Hebrew Roots' observance of Sukkot, the Feast of Tabernacles. For eight days we praise YHVH through our actions - prayer, song and dance, Bible study, feasting and fellowship. We hear from gifted speakers who teach us the ways and walk of YHVH, our Father, and who teach us the meaning of this very special time of year referred to by the ancient Jewish sages as "the Season of Our JOY". www.sooj.org

Shavuot/Shavot: See Feast of Weeks.

Sheep: The elect of God are called his sheep and His sons.

Straits: See Tishah B'Av.
The terms channel, pass, or passage can be synonymous and used interchangeably with strait, although each is sometimes differentiated with varying senses. -Wikipedia

Glossary of Terms

Tare: Chaff in this text refers to the unrighteous who rejected Jesus, the Son of God. Chaff/Tares are referenced in the bible in Matthew 13:24-40. The Sheep and the Goats or "the Judgement of the Nations" is a pronouncement of Jesus recorded in chapter 25 of the Gospel of Matthew, although unlike most parables it does not purport to relate a story of events happening to other characters.-Wikipedia

Tisha B'Av: marks the end of the three weeks between dire straits and is regarded as the saddest day in the Jewish calendar, and it is thus believed to be a day which is destined for tragedy.[2][3] Tisha B'Av falls in July or August in the Gregorian calendar. -Wikipedia

Tishah B'Av: (Hebrew: תִּשְׁעָה בְּאָב[a] Tīšʿā Bəʾāv; IPA: [tiʃa beʔav] (listen), lit. 'the ninth of Av') is an annual fast day in Judaism, on which a number of disasters in Jewish history occurred, primarily the destruction of both Solomon's Temple by the Neo-Babylonian Empire and the Second Temple by the Roman Empire in Jerusalem.

Tu B'Av: (Hebrew: ט"ו באב, lit. 'fifteenth of Av') is a minor Jewish holiday.[2] In modern-day Israel, it is celebrated as a holiday of love (חג האהבה Ḥag HaAhava).[3] According to the Mishna, Tu B'Av was a joyous holiday in the days of the Temple in Jerusalem, marking the beginning of the grape harvest.[4] On Yom Kippur and Tu B'Av, the unmarried girls of Jerusalem dressed in white garments and went out to dance in the vineyards.[5][2][6]
The Talmud states that there were no holy days as happy for the Jews as Tu B'Av and Yom Kippur.[7] The holiday celebrated the wood-offering brought in the Temple (see Nehemiah 13:31). -Wikipedia

Tu B'Shevat: A Tu B'Shevat seder is a festive ceremony, often accompanied by a meal featuring fruits in honor of the Jewish holiday of Tu B'Shevat. During the Middle Ages or possibly a little before that, this day started to be celebrated with a minor ceremony of eating fruits, since the Mishnah called it "Rosh Hashanah" ("New Year"), and that was later understood as being a time appropriate for celebration.-Wikipedia

Glossary of Terms

Wheat: Wheat in this text is refers to as the righteous Bride of Christ in the parable of Matthew 13:24.

Wheat harvest- Refer to Matthew 13:24-30. See Wheat. See Feast of Weeks. Harvest is the Bride of Christ who will be raptured when Christ Jesus Returns.

Wineskin: New Wine into Old Wineskins (οἶνον νέον εἰς ἀσκοὺς παλαιούς, lit.: New Wine into Old Bottles) is a parable of Jesus. It is found at Matthew 9:14-17, Mark 2:18-22 and Luke 5:33-39. -Wikipedia

And he spake also a parable unto them; No man putteth a piece of a new garment upon an old; if otherwise, then both the new maketh a rent, and the piece that was taken out of the new agreeth not with the old. And no man putteth new wine into old bottles; else the new wine will burst the bottles, and be spilled, and the bottles shall perish. But new wine must be put into new bottles; and both are preserved. No man also having drunk old wine straightway desireth new: for he saith, The old is better. Luke 5:36-39, KJV-Wikipedia

Yom Kippur (Atonement): The Day of Atonement (Leviticus 23:27-28), known in Hebrew as Yom Kippur (Heb. יוֹם הַכִּפּוּרִים, Yom ha-Kippurim – actual translation as "Day of the Atonements" or "Day of Coverings"), was the most solemn holy day of all the Israelite feasts and festivals, occurring once a year on the tenth day of Tishri, the seventh month of the Hebrew calendar.

In the Old Testament, the High Priest performed rituals with an atoning sacrifice for the sins of himself, his family, and the people on Yom Kippur (Day of Atonement). It is one of seven "appointed seasons of Elohim, holy convocations." - sabbathhouseinstitute.org